RAINTREE BIOGRAPHIES

Frank Lloyd Wright

Scott Ingram

Published by Raintree, a division of Reed Elsevier, Inc.

Project Editors: Marta Segal Block, Helena Attlee
Production Manager: Brian Suderski
Designed by Ian Winton

Planned and produced by Discovery Books

Library of Congress Cataloging-in-Publication Data:

Ingram, Scott (William Scott)
Frank Lloyd Wright / Scott Ingram.
p. cm. -- (Raintree biographies)
Summary: A biography of the innovative American architect
whose ideas influenced the direction of design in the twentieth century.
Includes bibliographical references and index.
ISBN 0-7398-6866-7 (HC), 1-4109-0068-1 (Pbk.)
1. Wright, Frank Lloyd, 1867-1959--Juvenile literature. 2. Ar-
chitects--United States--Biography--Juvenile literature. [1.
Wright, Frank Lloyd, 1867-1959. 2. Architects.] I. Title. II. Series.
NA737.W7I54 2003
720'.92--dc21
[B]

2002154987

Printed and bound in the United States
1 2 3 4 5 6 7 8 9 0 08 07 06 05 04 03

Acknowledgments
The publishers would like to thank the following for permission to reproduce their pictures:
Corbis: 8, 9, 10, 12, 14, 15, 19, 24, 26, 27, 28, 29; The Frank Lloyd Wright Foundation: 6, 7, 21;
The Hulton Archive: cover, 5, 18, 22; Jeffery Howe, Boston College: 4, 11, 13, 16, 17, 20, 23, 25.

Some words are shown in bold, **like this**.
You can find out what they mean by looking in the glossary.

CONTENTS

FALLINGWATER

In 1935, when Frank Lloyd Wright was almost 70 years old, he **designed** a house called Fallingwater. It became one of the most famous houses ever built. In 1938, when the building work was finished, photos of Fallingwater appeared in newspapers and magazines all over the world. When they saw the pictures, many people realized that Wright was one of America's greatest **architects**.

*Named the "greatest all-time work of American **architecture**," Fallingwater was a moment of triumph for Frank Lloyd Wright.*

Water Music

To Wright, the sound of the water falling was part of the music of nature: *"You listen to Fallingwater the way you listen to the quiet of the country,"* he said.

Part of the Landscape

Wright believed that buildings should appear to be a natural part of the **landscape** around them. His **masterpiece**, Fallingwater, seemed to be part of the forest around it. The concrete platforms on which the house stood echoed the sounds of water tumbling over the fall.

Fallingwater was built for the Kaufman family on wooded land in western Pennsylvania. The Kaufmans wanted the house to stand beside a waterfall on a creek. Wright soon let them know that he did not want to build a house beside the water. Instead, he wanted to build it over the waterfall!

Fallingwater was unlike any house that had ever been seen before. It was built on **concrete** platforms that appeared to float over the waterfall.

Frank Lloyd Wright continued to work until the end of his long life. Taken in 1950, this picture shows him at his desk, when he was almost 80 years old.

CHILDHOOD ON THE PRAIRIE

Frank Lloyd Wright was born on June 8, 1867, in the small farming town of Richland Center, Wisconsin. His father was a minister and a musician, and his mother a teacher.

Wright grew up surrounded by uncles, aunts, and cousins. This is a picture of his mother's family, the Lloyds.

Taliesin

Wright's grandparents came to Wisconsin from Wales, a part of Britain, during the 1860s. They settled about 40 miles (65 kilometers) west of Madison, where the steep hills rose from the flat land, reminding them of their homeland. They named the largest hill "Taliesin," the name of a famous Welsh poet. As a boy, Wright spent happy summers working at his uncle's farm, near Taliesin.

Wright's mother wanted her son to be an **architect** when he grew up and **design** buildings for a living. She hung pictures of some of the world's most famous buildings in his nursery. As soon as he could hold a pencil, he was taught to draw shapes such as circles, squares, and triangles. His mother also filled his playroom with glue and cardboard, so that he could make imaginary buildings.

When Wright was thirteen, the family settled in the town of Madison, Wisconsin, where he attended high school. At age fifteen, he was accepted as a student at the University of Wisconsin. A short time later, Wright's parents divorced, and he never saw his father again.

Frank Lloyd Wright never lost his love of the land. As an elderly man, he continued to work on the farm at Taliesin.

YOUNG ARCHITECT

In 1887, twenty-year-old Wright left college to become an **architect**. He moved to Chicago, Illinois, and soon found a job working for Louis Sullivan, one of the most famous architects in the United States. Sullivan's buildings in downtown Chicago were widely admired as some of the best examples of a new **structure** called a "**skyscraper**."

Sullivan was both a boss and a friend to Wright, who called him his "beloved master."

Rebuilding Chicago

In the mid-1800s, Chicago was a wealthy place. In 1871, however, a huge fire killed 300 people and destroyed thousands of buildings. This **tragedy** drew architects such as Louis Sullivan to Chicago, where they worked to rebuild the city. By 1890, there were dozens of new skyscrapers.

Wright quickly became Sullivan's chief **draftsperson**. He completed Sullivan's plans for stores, office buildings, and **auditoriums**, calling himself "the pencil in Sullivan's hands."

After several years, Sullivan put Wright in charge of his company's home **design** department. Soon, Wright began to develop ideas unlike any Sullivan had ever seen. The houses had low roofs, open rooms flowing into one another, and a fireplace in the center of the home. Sullivan soon asked Wright to design a home for his own family.

Sullivan's Auditorium Building had an open-air room at its center. It was considered one of the most beautiful buildings in Chicago.

THE BOOTLEG HOMES

By age 25, Wright was chief **architect** at Sullivan and Adler, the largest architectural company in Chicago. Wright was soon well known. Many people admired his work and asked him to **design** houses for them. Taking on work outside the company was called "bootlegging," and it was against the rules, but Wright had debts to pay. He took on private jobs, and was fired as a result.

These crowded Chicago streets, photographed at the beginning of the twentieth century, would have been familiar to Frank Lloyd Wright.

Regrets

In later years, Wright regretted the loss of his friendship with Sullivan, the man who had trained him in the basic ideas of **architecture**. *"The bad end to a glorious relationship,"* Wright wrote, *"has been a dark shadow . . . all the days of my life."*

Three Bootleg houses that Wright designed while working for Sullivan still stand in Oak Park. This is Walter Gale House, built in 1893.

Three of the houses that Wright designed while he was working for Sullivan and Adler can still be seen today in Oak Park, Illinois, a wealthy suburb of Chicago. By looking at them, we can understand Wright's first ideas about the design of houses. Some features of the Bootleg homes were completely new. For example, they had round front rooms and very long chimneys.

THE PRAIRIE STYLE

After he was fired, Wright set up an office in his home in Oak Park, Illinois. The house is now a museum that is visited by thousands of tourists each year. From 1893 to 1901, more than 40 Wright houses were built there in an original **design** that came to be known as his **Prairie** Style.

Wright experimented with many of his own ideas when building this house for himself in Oak Park.

Until Wright began to design houses, most buildings had tended to stand out from their surroundings. The Prairie homes were different. With their low, overhanging roofs and rows of small windows, the houses blended in with the **landscape**.

The inside of Wright's Prairie Style houses was also designed in a new way. Instead of breaking up the space into the usual small, boxes, he used glass doors between the rooms, and joined them around a central fireplace. Chairs, sofas, and tables were built out from the wall, so that much of the floor area was open and seemed larger than it was.

An example of Wright's Prairie Style, Nathan Moore House was built in Oak Park in 1895, and rebuilt in 1924.

WEALTH AND FAME

Wright continued to develop his ideas, and by the early 1900s, he was one of the most famous **architects** in the United States. He invented a new word to describe the shape of his buildings, which he called "**streamlined**."

The **Prairie** Style was one of the first truly American building designs. American architects used to imitate European styles, but now they began to study Wright's ideas. They soon adopted his approach, creating simple houses that seemed to grow out of their natural surroundings.

With its strong colors and unpainted furniture, Wright's own studio at Taliesin is a good example of Craftsman Movement style.

Wright's houses were built from local materials and filled with plain, unpainted furniture. Walls were painted in rich earth colors instead of being covered with bright wallpaper. Wright's work was part of a new style of **design** known as Arts and **Crafts**, or the **Craftsman** Movement.

A typical example of the bungalow style, Gamble House was built in California in 1908. Wright's influence was clear in this design and many others like it.

Bungalows

Named after Indian houses with wide porches — or *bangala* — bungalows were one of the most popular buildings of the early twentieth century. With low roofs and rooms running into each other, their design reflected Wright's ideas. Bungalows were popular in places with a warm climate, and thousands were built from "Craftsman Kits" that sold for less than $1,000.

TALIESIN TRAGEDY

By 1911 Wright had made enough money to return to Wisconsin, and buy the land on which his uncle's farm once stood. Using **designs** drawn very early in his career, he built a school, a cabin, a church, and a windmill. In 1912 Wright designed a house, a studio, and a farmyard. He named his new home Taliesin, in honor of both his grandfather, and his mother, who had encouraged him to become an **architect**.

Feeling at Home

"Taliesin! I am away from it, like some rubber band, stretched out but ready to snap back immediately, [when] the pull is relaxed or released. I get back to it, happy to be home again."

Frank Lloyd Wright

This is the house at Taliesin, which overlooked land once farmed by Wright's grandfather.

The dream of Taliesin turned to a nightmare in 1914, when a worker set the buildings on fire, killing seven people. Wright survived and rebuilt Taliesin, but the crime was the greatest **tragedy** of his life.

Wright in Wisconsin

In 1915 Wright designed this unusual building in Milwaukee, Wisconsin. It was called the Richards Duplex. It was made from wood that was pre-cut into the correct shape. The rooms inside could be put together in several different ways. Duplex buildings were like the blocks that Wright played with as a child.

THE WAITER'S TRAY

After the shocking events of 1914, Wright found it difficult to work at Taliesin. When he was asked to **design** a hotel in Tokyo, Japan, in 1916, he eagerly agreed. Between 1916 and 1922 Wright lived in Japan and designed the Imperial Hotel in downtown Tokyo.

The entrance to the Imperial Hotel in Tokyo. Sadly, the building was demolished in 1968 to make way for a taller and more modern structure. Parts of the original building were taken to a memorial park.

Wright's biggest challenge was to make a building strong enough to survive earthquakes. Most new buildings in Tokyo had large **foundation** stones buried deep in the earth. The weight was carried by these supports at the sides of the building. As usual, Wright's design was different. He was inspired by the sight of a waiter carrying a tray. The man's arm was held above his head, and he balanced the center of the tray on his fingertips. By using dozens of short supports at the center of the building, Wright created the same effect.

The Great Kanto Earthquake

On September 1, 1923, Tokyo was struck by the Great Kanto earthquake. Thousands died, but Wright's Imperial Hotel suffered only slight damage. Not long after returning to the U.S., Wright received a telegram from the hotel's owner: "Hotel stands undamaged as monument of your **genius**. Congratulations. Okura."

Wright's Imperial Hotel was one of the few buildings to remain standing in Tokyo after the devastating earthquake of 1923 reduced much of the town to rubble.

An Uncertain Time

In 1922 Wright spent a year in Los Angeles, California, where he studied the use of a new building material called **concrete**. Until the 1920s, most buildings were made of wood, stone, brick, or steel. Concrete, a mix of gravel and **cement**, could be shaped into blocks before it hardened. Wright used blocks held together with steel rods to build four houses in the hills around Los Angeles.

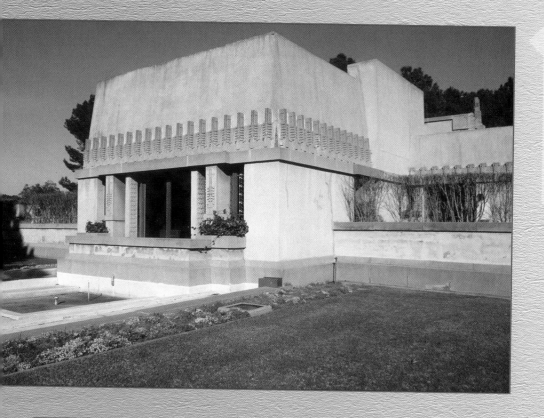

Named Hollyhock House, this is a fine example of a concrete house designed by Wright and built in Los Angeles.

Designs for a Landscape

During his time in California, Wright drew many **designs** for the kind of settlements that are known today as **resorts** or **developments**. Although none of them was ever built, they were the first ideas for building on this scale.

This photograph was taken at Taliesin on Christmas Eve, 1924.

In 1923 Wright returned to Taliesin for the first time in seven years. In 1924 both his mother and Louis Sullivan, the man that he still called his "master," died. A year later, Taliesin was again damaged by fire and had to be rebuilt. Wright had borrowed a great deal of money, and he was unable to repay the loan. He was forced to move out of Taliesin by the bank that had loaned him the money.

STARTING SCHOOL

In 1927, at the age of 60, Wright began to write the story of his life. In October 1932 it was published, and it sold thousands of copies. The book earned Wright the money that he so badly needed, and attracted people to Taliesin. He soon realized that many people wanted to be his students, and so in 1933 he started a school at Taliesin. Wright's students studied **architecture**, and also construction, farming, and nature. Several years later, Wright and his first students **designed** and built Taliesin West in Arizona, where he could teach during winter months.

Wright was a popular teacher. Here he pauses to speak to one of his students in the classroom at Taliesin West in Arizona.

The Usonian Home

Most of his **clients** were wealthy people, but in 1935 Wright designed this plain, inexpensive wooden house for everyday, working Americans. He called it the Usonian Home. It had pre-built walls and an open floor plan. Wright added a covered area for the family car, for which he invented the word "carport."

Herbert Jacobs House, built in Madison, Wisconsin in 1936, was one of Wright's Usonian Homes. It could be built from a kit for about $5,500.

Wright hired several assistants. With their help, he was able to take on much more work. He soon became famous again. In many ways, he was even more famous than before. Two of Wright's best-known buildings are from this time period. One was Fallingwater in Pennsylvania, and the other was the Johnson Wax Building in Wisconsin.

A Varied Portfolio

Wright's houses and his other buildings are his best-known work. Some people do not realize that he also spent a great deal of time **designing** objects to go inside his **clients**' homes. Wright's furniture, lamps, and other kinds of lights are now highly prized by collectors all over the world.

Frank Lloyd Wright did some of his most interesting design work using the first shapes that his mother had taught him as a child: circles, triangles, squares, and rectangles. He enjoyed using those shapes in window designs and developed many ideas in the windows of his own home.

Lights designed by Wright to hang in Oak Park's Unity Temple.

Over his long career, Wright designed a number of chapels, churches, and synagogues. Some of these buildings were revolutionary. Unity Temple in Oak Park, Illinois, for example, was one of the first buildings ever to be constructed from concrete poured into molds.

The Greek Orthodox Church that he designed in Wauwatosa, Wisconsin, is another unusual **structure**. It is a circular building.

*The brightly colored **facade** of Wright's Greek Orthodox Church, built in 1956.*

FINAL YEARS

During the last years of his life, Wright was busier than ever. He gave interviews on radio and television, **designed** more than 450 houses and some of his best-known public buildings, such as the Price Tower in Oklahoma and the Marin County Civic Center in California.

When Wright designed the Marin County Civic Center he was in his late 80s.

Perhaps the most famous building of Wright's final years was the Solomon R. Guggenheim Museum in New York City. Wright did not like New York City because he found it too crowded. He chose a site for the museum near Central Park, the largest green area in the city. His circular, spiral design was so unusual that he had to fight city leaders and many New Yorkers for permission to build the museum.

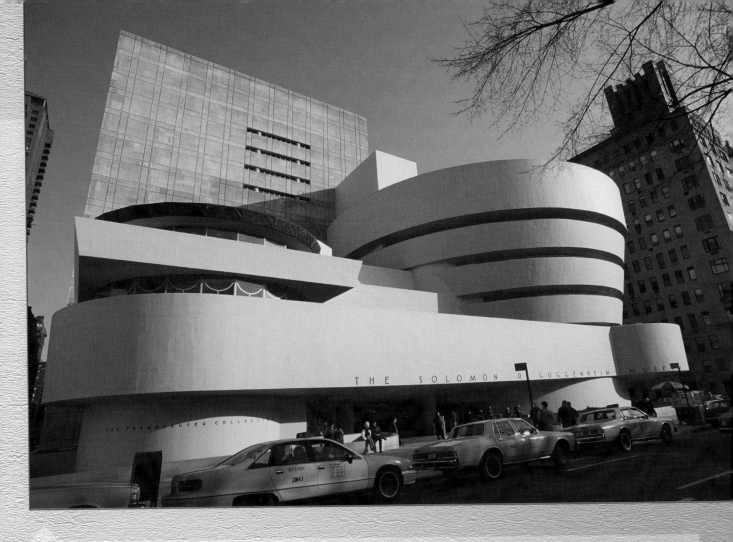

When it was first built, Wright's Guggenheim Museum was very surprising. Now it is one of the most popular buildings in New York City.

Construction of the Guggenheim had just begun when Wright turned 90 in 1957. He died in April 1959 in Phoenix, Arizona. The Guggenheim Museum opened a few months later.

UNITY CHAPEL

Wright died near Taliesin West in Arizona. His final resting place, however, was the land that he loved throughout his life, Taliesin in Wisconsin. He was buried next to his mother. Beside the cemetery stands the chapel, Wright's first building, which he designed when he was twenty years old.

WRIGHT'S LEGACY

Although it might seem as if Frank Lloyd Wright lived long ago, many of his ideas are still part of our lives today. Any houses built in the ranch or bungalow style, with low roofs overhanging a wide porch, are inspired by Wright's original ideas. Homes built with carports or skylights are another example of Wright's influence, and so are houses that have open-plan rooms and built-in furniture. In fact, any home that has a living room at all is using an idea first **designed** by Wright.

The inside of the Guggenheim, with its spiral walkway, is still very striking today, more than 40 years after it was designed.

Built in 1927, Taliesin West in Arizona is a mixture of stone, metal, concrete and glass. Its bold shapes are echoed by the triangle-shaped stretch of water in front of the building.

Wright's designs changed the **architecture** of the United States. During his 70-year career, he designed over 1,000 houses, offices, churches, schools, libraries, bridges, museums, and other buildings. More than 500 designs were built, and over 400 of them still stand.

Wright's designs for both the outside and the inside of living and working spaces was important to American life. Many people might agree with an art expert who calls Wright, "the greatest artist this country had produced."

TIMELINE

1867 - June 8, – Frank Lloyd Wright is born in Richland Center, Wisconsin

1880 – Wright family moves to Madison, Wisconsin

1883 – Wright enters the University of Wisconsin

1885 – Wright's parents divorce

1887 – Moves to Chicago to become chief draftsperson at Sullivan and Adler

1889 – Designs his own home in Oak Park, Illinois

1890-1892 – Designs the Bootleg homes

1893 – Opens his own practice in Chicago

1911 – Buys land near the family farms and begins building a new home and studio he names "Taliesin"

1914 – A worker kills seven people after setting fire to Taliesin

1916 – Sails to Japan to begin work on the Imperial Hotel

1922 – Returns to America from Japan and opens an office in Los Angeles

1923 – Designs Lake Tahoe Resort, Lake Tahoe, California

1923 – Wright moves to Taliesin. Wright's mother and Louis Sullivan die

1924 – Second major fire occurs at Taliesin

1932 – Wright's autobiography is published

1933 – Establishes a school at Taliesin

1935 – Wright designs Fallingwater and first Usonian home

1936 – Designs Johnson Wax Factory, Wisconsin

1937 – Purchases land in Arizona and begins construction of Taliesin West

1938 – Fallingwater completed

1949 – Wins gold medal of the American Institute of Architecture

1953 – Designs Price Tower, Bartlesville, Oklahoma

1956 – Final plan for the Guggenheim Museum is approved

1959 – Frank Lloyd Wright dies in Arizona. The Guggenheim Museum opens.

GLOSSARY

architect person who designs houses or other buildings

architecture process of designing buildings

auditorium room or building used for public gatherings

autobiography story of someone's own life

cement mixture of lime and clay used in building

client person who buys or uses the services of another

concrete strong building material made by mixing cement with sand or gravel

craft job that needs skill, especially with the hands

craftsperson person who is especially skilled at a craft

design to create or construct. The plan for an object or building is called a design.

development an area of land used for building houses, stores, factories, etc.

draftsperson person who draws plans and sketches

facade front of a building

foundation base which supports a structure built above it

genius somebody with exceptional talent

landscape scenery or natural surroundings

legacy something handed down by a previous generation

masterpiece work or high achievement created with great skill

portfolio collection of work

prairie flat grassland with few trees or other plants

resort place where people go on vacatiion

skyscraper very tall, narrow building

streamlined having a smooth shape

structure something that has been constructed, such as a building

tragedy disastrous event

FURTHER READING

Boulton, Alexander O. *Frank Lloyd Wright Architect: A Picture Biography.* New York: Rizzoli International Publications, 1993.

Rubin, Goldman, Susan. *There Goes the Neighborhood: 10 Buildings People Loved to Hate.* New York: Holiday House, 2001.

Wilkinson, Philip. *Building.* New York: Dorling Kindersley Publishing, 2000.

INDEX